Smoking Meat For Beginners

The Ultimate Guide For Getting Started With Irresistible Recipes

Tony A. Chagnon

Smoking Meat For Beginners: The Ultimate Guide For Getting Started With Irresistible Recipes

Table of Contents

1 - Introduction

Smoking is a technique that early civilizations used to preserve food, particularly meats. Properly smoked food usually lasts for a long time hence people survived harsh seasons such as winter. Nowadays, smoking is more of a culinary method rather than a means of preservation. The art of smoking was kept alive by food connoisseurs due to the unique and authentic taste that it offers.

Smoking meats is not for the faint of heart. It requires the ability to pick a quality meat, test unorthodox cooking methods and use make-shift materials.

Smoking food will be a test of your patience and skills because it won't be easy for a beginner. But, once you learn the craft, it will be enjoyable and rewarding.

2 - Why Smoke Your Food?

Smoking enhances the flavor of the food, especially in terms of meat. Smoking also makes the meat tender and succulent due to the long cooking process.

Smoking also improves a person's cooking capabilities as it expands one's knowledge of cooking techniques, types of meat cuts, forms of fuel, and smoking equipment.

3 – Starting the Your Pit Master Journey

Now that you are convinced to take your meat-cooking skills to the next level, the continuation is to find your equipment of choice.

Coal Grill Smoking

As an exploratory beginner, it is a good idea to work with what is accessible to you. Most households have ready-to-use coal grills so take advantage of it.

Set up your charcoal grill as you normally would. Pile your coals on one side or divide them into two batches and place them on either side of the grill.

Next, place a pan of liquid on the drip pan to add moisture to the food during the smoking process. You may opt to use fruit juices like apple extract for additional flavor.

Pick a type of fragrant wood so it releases a good smell when put in the fire. Choose wood chips or wood chunks and soak them in water for at least 30 minutes before placing them on the embers. Light your coals until they are hot enough then put the soaked wood on top to create smoke.

Place the food on the grill and leave them there until they are well-done. Leave an opening in between the grill and lid to create a ventilation for the smoke.

Gas Grill Smoking

If you find charcoal grills a bit tricky, then opt for a gas stove for smoking instead. The process is similar to setting up a charcoal grill.

Place your previously soaked wood chips on a metal pan before putting them over the fire. Place them on one side of the burner and preheat the food items on high heat for 20 minutes.

Once the stove is warm enough for cooking, place your food opposite the wood and close the lid, but leave an opening to regulate the fumes.

Store-Bought Smoker

If you have extra money then you can buy a barbecue smoker that uses wood, charcoal or pellets as the heat source. Unlike the makeshift smoking equipment, a real smoking machine can produce authentic, deeply infused smokiness to your dishes. It also cooks food thoroughly and evenly at high temperatures through heat distribution on the smoker's surface. You can cook fall-off the bones meat without the fuss.

Types of Smokers

There are two types of smoking device: the wet and dry smokers. Opt for the method that best suits your environment.

A Wet Smoker is a beginner's buddy. This cylindrical water smoker is a type of wet smoker that has three racks. The bottom rack holds the charcoal, the middle rack has the liquid, and the top rack holds the meats. The design basically steams the meat while smoking it.

The Vertical Wet Smoker is a kind of wet smoker that is less costly and beginner-friendly. These have wide vents for better air circulation and heat production.

A Dry Smoker is an indirect way to cook food using smoldering firewood to slowly cook meat and infuse the smoky flavor.

Electric Smokers are smokers which use electrical energy to heat up a rod that ignites the wood to bring forth smoke.

These types of smokers are easier to regulate because of the built-in dial for temperature adjustment. Unfortunately, the electric smoker also costs a fortune and delivers the least amount of smoke, hence it is only ideal for small, enclosed spaces.

4 - Off to a Fiery Start

After choosing your smoking instrument, the succeeding step is to select your fuel. Enumerated below are the most common smoking fuels that pit masters use.

Types of Fuel for Smoking Meats

- Wood

  Wood is the popular choice for meat smokers. This is the cheapest, most accessible, and novice-friendly fuel. The quality of wood determines the richness of the meat's flavor so the higher its quality, the tastier the meats.

  There are several kinds of wood that match specific food groups:

  Cherry and Oakwood are good for pork, beef, seafood, and chicken.

  Alder and Mulberry are great for chicken, seafood, and pork, but are not fit for smoking beef.

  Hickory, Mesquite, and Walnut work best with pork and beef, but not with chicken and seafood.

Peach and Pearwood compliment chicken and pork, but not beef and seafood.

Pecan wood is good for chicken, pork, and beef, but not for seafood.

When choosing your wood, remember that chicken and seafood absorb flavor easily so fragrant and light wood is suitable for these. On the other hand, wood with strong aroma is perfect for pork and beef which do not absorb flavor too much.

Size and Form of Wood

- Wood Pieces

Determining your wood medium is dependent on your cooking time. Generally, if you want to slow cook your meats for a long time then opt for the thickest cut, which is called the Wood Chunks. They last for almost a day and give out more helpful smoke. These will produce the most tender meat of all. To make them last longer, presoak in water at least 30 minutes prior to use.

For a moderate cooking time, Wood Chips are your

best friend. These last for a few hours and provide ample smoke. Other than livestock, these bits are also good for fish and vegetables, which can only be smoked for a shorter time.

If you only prefer a hint of smoke on your meats, then Wood Pellets are your best bet. They burn fast so preparation must be done quickly. Soaking them beforehand is still essential. This merely aids in adding smoky flavor to the meat rather than tenderizing.

- Charcoal

Another fuel that you can use to smoke your meats is charcoal. Unlike wood, charcoal doesn't have a distinct smell or flavor because their main purpose is to provide intense fire.

If you want a wood-like alternative then go for the Lump Charcoal. Lump charcoal comes from real wood burnt to become charcoal. It has a subtle smokiness and stays longer than commercial camping coals. Though it is initially more expensive, it saves you money in the long run because a small amount goes a long way. The high temperatures that they emit make them more efficient in softening meat cartilage. You can buy Lump coals at outdoor recreation stores in the form of black wood blocks.

Briquette charcoal is your basic, commonly accessible charcoal. These are sawdust -like materials made of coal dust, wood chips, paper or peat and other flammable items pressed together to form a piece. These are relatively lighter than lump charcoals and provide consistent temperature. They are also cheaper and burn much longer than lump coals.

Less supervision is also necessary for Briquette Charcoals. However, the unpleasant chemical smell they produce makes them less appealing to consumers. The chemical residues that the ingredients contain and the large amount of ash after being consumed is another concern.

- Coal

Coal is neither your friend nor foe when it comes to smoking meats. It doesn't offer much flavor nor can it withstand the long cooking process. But it can be your last option when the other materials are unavailable.

Tips

Whatever heat source you use, make sure to avoid using lighter fluid or any self-combustive material to ignite the fire. The chemicals will produce an unpleasant aftertaste in the meat products.

Also, regularly check your fuel source, add more fuel to maintain the heat, and replace burnt items as soon as possible to get a clean smoky taste. Change your charcoal or wood every few hours.

Be sure to keep the temperature between 200-250 degrees and use a cooking thermometer to maintain your heat levels.

Ventilation is crucial during the smoking process. Stagnant air in the smoker will raise the heat and burn the food from the inside. It might also give you a burnt, ashy taste. Remember to provide enough airing for your meats during the smoking process.

5 - Knowing Your Meats and How to Smoke Them

Now that you know the various kinds of equipment, learning about different meats and the best meat cuts for smoking purposes is your next agenda.

Seafood is a rare choice for smoking due to the limited kinds of sea fauna fit for smoking. But the most smoke-worthy is the Salmon. This fatty fish is good for smoking due to the fat it contains that serves as a buffer in the cooking process. Salmon also releases a rich flavor when smoked compared to other fishes. If you're feeling adventurous, try cold smoking a salmon instead.

Other seafood to consider are lobster, St. Peter's fish, and trout.

Sausages are well-smoked appetizers for food enthusiasts. Pick sausages with a balance of lean and fat and those with a heat-resistant casing. Sausages are best cooked at 160 degrees because bacteria affect ground meat faster than cut portions of meat. Smoke the cold sausages at 30-60 minutes only. Don't over-smoke them.

Lamb is a delicious meat that you can smoke. Leg of lamb

can be a tricky delicacy because of its natural uneven cut, but a slow cooking process is ideal for this meat. Boneless cuts can be reduced into small pieces and cooked one at a time. It is easier to manage the temperature for bite-size meats rather than huge or whole pieces.

The shoulder cut of a lamb has high-fat content, which is perfect for smoking. This part needs to be cooked creatively because of the taste and toughness of the meat. Another challenging aspect of lamb is the rarity and high price.

Poultry is best as a whole hen or quarters. Whole meats are cheap and easy to prepare. The bird is fairly small so it can be cooked well while retaining the moisture of the meat. Chicken quarters are large portions of dark meat which greatly absorb flavor so they are great for practicing pur-poses.

Turkey is a poultry alternative that can be cooked just as beautifully.

Pork shoulder or Boston Butt is one of the easiest cuts to handle in swine. It releases fat overtime and coats itself nat-urally, so basting is seldom needed as moisture is locked in the meat. Mistakes are uncommon for this cut because it cooks evenly. Ribs, on the other hand, are one of the staples for professional meat smokers. These are very easy to work with, less expensive, and effortless to find. Ham is another cut to experiment with.

Beef Brisket is at the top of the smoked meats list since it is easy to find and savory when smoked. It has a thick fat layer so slow-cooking is ideal and it finishes with a pinkish meat when well-done. The prime ribs are a worthy cut for smoking, it's quite flavorful but rather difficult to cook for an amateur, so it is normally at the bottom of a novice's list.

In addition to meats, vegetables and cheese can also be smoked for a few hours. They can serve as your side dishes and can be cooked together with premium meats. These may also be presented as the main course for vegans.

6 - Preparing Your Meats

After choosing your meat, flavoring is the next step. There are three common ways to infuse flavor into meats: brining, marinade or dry rub.

A dry rub is normally used for thick cuts of meat like steak and ribs. It is a powdered combination of spices and salt. It is applied to the meat prior to cooking and made to rest for a few minutes.

Marinades are applicable to light and soft meats like chicken and seafood. These meats absorb flavor quickly and should ideally be left overnight in the fridge.

For brisket and other beef cuts, score the meat a few times so the marinade can seep through. Let the meat treat for at least 30 minutes and then drained. Leave it at room temperature before being cooked.

Brining is a step toward curing meats like ham and poultry. Brining retains the liquid content of the meat. Sodium chloride ions interact with the meat proteins, which makes them loose and moist during the cooking period. If you plan to brine, mix the brine and coat your meat generously, then leave them to rest for 8 hours. For optimum fluid retention, soak your meats in a brine solution for 10-12 hours prior to smoking or opt to prepare the meat in the evening so you can leave it overnight.

For a fancy brine base, add some herbs and spices to the mix. Add three tablespoons of salt to one quart of water and add your preferred condiments.

Brining is a good moisture-retaining method, but it also makes the meats saltier so add sweeteners like sugar, honey or molasses to reduce the saltiness.

Flavoring before smoking is a step that adds another taste dimension to your food aside from the smoke. It is also a nice precautionary step to put your mind at ease instead of thinking if the food tastes great or not.

Let Your Meat Rest

Setting your meat makes a huge difference when smoking. Resting the meat allows it to reach room temperature, which means it will cook evenly during the smoking process. Leave the meat to rest for a minimum of 1 1/2 -2 hours for moderately cut meats. Thicker cuts need additional time for resting.

7 - Let the Smoking Begin!

Let us now start with the most important part, smoking your meats.

Compute the length of your cooking time.

A regular meat smoking session is usually a minimum of six hours and can last up to eight hours or more depending on the type of meat, the cut, and the temperature of the smoker.

Pork and beef ribs commonly cook for about 8 hours while a large, thick brisket can last up to 22 hours in the smoker.

Planning ahead and double checking your recipe is important in achieving delicious food.

Remember that slow and low temperatures won't rupture the cell walls of the meat making the food more succulent. It also makes hard tendons and collagen into gelatinous substance without affecting the meat's quality.

Place your meats on the smoker

Set your meat on top of the grill or on a shallow aluminum

tray or any container where the smoke can envelop it. Avoid wrapping the meats in aluminum foil as it will not produce a good smokey flavor.

The positioning of the meat is relevant to the type of meat as well. For instance, a brisket should be placed fat side up and lean side down so the fat coats the entire meat when it melts.

Never expose your meat directly over the fire. Smoking is an indirect cooking method so the heat source must be placed a little far from the meat. Again, slow cooking is the key to a great smoked meat.

Basting the Meats

Moisture is very important in the smoking process. You don't want a tough, cracked, flavorless meat. Basting maintains the moisture level of your food. Not all recipes need the meat to drenched, big cuts like ribs and brisket usually do. If the meat is not over the fire and is cooked slowly, they will surely come out moist and tender.

If you smoke big batches of meat, you can use a barbecue mop to spread water all over the meat or use fruit juices for added sweetness or tang. Water, vinegar, and spices also make a basic baste.

Put a Lid on It

Some recipes require alternately covering the meats when being smoked. The 3-2-1 process is a popular smoking technique that requires the meat to smoke for three hours. Next, it should be left covered for the succeeding two hours, finally, leave the meat open for the last hour of cooking. To elaborate, the 3-hour smoking infuses the smoke in the food, the 2-hour covering period is to raise the internal temperature of the meats. Lastly, the final uncovered hour creates a good crusting for the meats.

Remove the meat

A meat thermometer is a good investment if you want to smoke correctly. A meat thermometer can easily determine if the meat is cooked properly or not. Poultry is cooked when it reaches 165 degrees. While pork and ground meats are done at 160 degrees. Steaks, roasts, and chops are good at 145 degrees.

Check for The Presence of "Smoke Ring"

One of the best indicators of a nicely smoked meat is the

smoke ring. It is a chemical reaction between the nitric acid in the meat and smoke. A pinkish ring forms just below the outer crust when the smoking process is successful.

8 - Conclusion

Smoking meats is definitely a labor of love. Smoking demands patience and culinary dedication. Bear in mind that a professional meat smoker was also once a beginner who persevered to master the art of smoking meats. Being a pit master is not for the weak of heart. It entails the studying of meat structure, experimenting with cooking methods and cooking aids.

Smoking is a marriage of science and intuition. It involves precision and order with regards to the preparation, but it needs the chef's good instincts to produce delicious food with good presentation. Remember that a pit master is once a novice who just refused to give up.

Thank You

As we reach the end of this book, I want to say thanks for reading this book.

I want to get this information out to as many people as possible. If you found this book helpful, I would greatly appreciate you leaving me a review. This helps others find the book as well.

Disclaimer

This document is geared towards providing exact and reliable information in regards to the topic and issue covered. The publication is sold on the idea that the publisher is not required to render an accounting, officially permitted, or otherwise, qualified services. If advice is necessary, legal, financial, medical or professional, a practiced individual in the profession should be ordered.

This information is not presented by a financial or medical practitioner and is for entertainment, educational and informational purposes only. The content is not intended as a substitute for professional medical advice, diagnosis, or treatment. Always seek the advice of your physician or other qualified health care provider with any questions you may have regarding a medical condition. Never disregard professional medical advice or delay in seeking it because of something you have read.

The information provided herein is stated to be truthful and consistent, in that any liability, in terms of inattention or otherwise, by any usage or abuse of any policies, processes, or directions contained within is the solitary and utter responsibility of the recipient reader. Under no circumstances will any legal responsibility or blame be held against the

DISCLAIMER

publisher for any reparation, damages, or monetary loss due to the information herein, either directly or indirectly.

Last Updated: 28.Jun.2018